# DYSFUNCTIONAL FAMILY
## Making Peace with Your Past

JUNE HUNT

HENDRICKSON PUBLISHERS   ROSE PUBLISHING

Dysfunctional Family: Making Peace with Your Past
Copyright © 2014 Hope For The Heart
Aspire Press is an imprint of
Rose Publishing, LLC
P.O. Box 3473
Peabody, Massachusetts 01961-3473 USA
www.hendricksonrose.com

The views and opinions expressed in this book are those of the author(s) and do not necessarily express the views of Rose Publishing, nor is this book intended to be a substitute for mental health treatment or professional counseling.

The information in this resource is intended as guidelines for healthy living. Please consult qualified medical, legal, pastoral, and psychological professionals regarding individual concerns.

For more information on Hope For The Heart, visit www.hopefortheheart.org or call 1-800-488-HOPE (4673).

Printed in the United States of America

December 2017, 5th printing

# CONTENTS

# Dear friend,

Quite frankly, someone took the *fun* out of my dys*fun*ctional family! In truth, my childhood was filled with severely painful secrets that—by virtue of an unspoken code called "family loyalty"—I was not to tell. And tell, *I did not*!

My father was a powerful man—double my mother's age—who maintained three families at the same time. Following the death of his first wife, we moved into his huge house. (I'd just turned 12.) Eleven months later, my parents married and sometime after, I began to be called "June Hunt." Prior to that, my mother, three siblings, and I convincingly wore the fictitious last name of "Wright." (What a play on words!)

Such deceit might seem unthinkable to someone raised differently, but bear in mind: Children grow up believing that whatever they experience is *normal* (no matter how abnormal). However, *their normal isn't normal*! And lacking a frame of reference, they assume everyone else is treated the same way ... at least for a while.

The inevitable question is: What happens when children raised in dysfunctional families grow up and move into the real world? Additionally, do damaged relationship patterns vanish quickly like a porch light in a rearview mirror? The simple answer is *No*. Instead, it's common to carry dysfunction from our "family of origin" right into new relationships—with classmates and roommates, employers and employees, friends and family, and a whole new generation of children.

Often this dysfunction surfaces with different looks—like having a "victim mentality," always feeling powerless, becoming a people pleaser, or violating one's own values. Gradually, an insidious lie spreads slowly into the heart like cancer: "I can't change what I am today because of my unchangeable past."

In absolute honesty, for years I felt powerless. I became a people pleaser, at times saying *yes* when I should have said *no*. I sincerely assumed I had no choice. Looking back, I had no idea that these negative patterns were born and bred during my early dysfunctional days.

Clearly, when I was a child I had no choice about much that was wrong. But when I became a young adult, I *did* have a choice. I *could* say *no*, but I *did not* change. I stayed stuck in those destructive dysfunctional patterns.

Eventually, as I applied what Jesus said, the truth set me *free*. The apostle Paul said, *"When I was a child, I spoke as a child, I understood as a child, I thought as a child; but when I became a man, I put away childish things"* (1 Corinthians 13:11 NKJV).

I needed to acknowledge: "I'm no longer a child." I *can* change—and I *did* change. And if *I* could change, anyone can change!

Regardless of your unchangeable past, *you, too, can change*. The key thought is found in grasping what it means to be a part of the family of God. The heavenly Father is not a dysfunctional father—He is a perfect, nurturing Father.

And when you entrust your life to Christ, not only does He adopt you into His family, He also puts Christ *in* you! Yes, the Bible reveals that the secret to your success is " ... *Christ in you, the hope of glory*" (Colossians 1:27).

Christ on the *inside* changes us—from the inside out. We no longer have to live feeling powerless, feeling desperate for approval, needing to please people, needing to fix people. Through the power of Christ, dysfunctional patterns can be broken.

Although you can't change your past, you can change your *attitude* about your past, and you can change your future by becoming the person God created you to be.

If you have experienced the pain of family dysfunction and desire to be made whole, recognize that you are holding the keys to your healing—here within these pages. No matter how troubled your past, no matter how turbulent your present, God has a plan for your future.

Our Lord speaks this truth so clearly, *"I know the plans I have for you ... plans to prosper you and not to harm you, plans to give you hope and a future"* (Jeremiah 29:11).

God promises if you follow His truths for wholeness, you will have a transformed life.

Don't be a prisoner of your past. Ultimately, with the power of Christ in you, your past will never control you.

Yours in the Lord's hope,

June Hunt

# DYSFUNCTIONAL FAMILY
## Making Peace with Your Past

Cathey Brown knows about dysfunctional families. She has immersed herself into thousands of them.

As an adult child of two alcoholics, Cathey is keenly aware of the sizeable swath of dysfunction that can sweep through families, consuming and crippling them when chemical dependence reigns in a home. Therefore, she has devoted her life to reaching struggling children, teaching invaluable life skills and instilling a sense of significance in them despite the most dysfunctional of families.

Cathey is founder of Rainbow Days, which has provided support groups for nearly 65,000 children since its inception. "I consider the work I do with Rainbow Days to be my calling and one of the main reasons God put me on earth," Cathey reflects. "I feel very blessed to do something that I enjoy, that utilizes my strengths and helps make a difference in the lives of children."[1]

Cathey's heart resembles the heart of the apostle Paul ...

" ... by this kind of hard work we must help
the weak, remembering the words
the Lord Jesus himself said:
'It is more blessed to give than to receive.'"
(Acts 20:35)

# DEFINITIONS

*On the outside, they look so picture perfect.*

Cathey Brown is raised in a traditional family, each member assuming the public role that communicates normalcy, congeniality, and the classic message: "We've got it all together, everything is great within the walls of our house."[2]

But behind closed doors things are falling apart. Cathey's father suddenly becomes verbally abusive and sometimes even physically violent, a transformation in behavior that terrifies Cathey and shatters her sense of security. Years pass before she connects her parents' arguments and meltdown of emotions to alcohol. Somehow Cathey always feels at fault for the family's dysfunction, and a sense of inadequacy and powerlessness swells within her spirit.[3]

She strives to compensate by overachieving, avowing to attain perfection and gain significance through top-notch grades in school and commendable extracurricular activities. Cathey feels she can control these areas, but the truth is that her chaotic home life is controlling her.[4]

Scripture gives direction about *who*, not what, should be controlling our minds ...

> " ... the mind governed by
> the Spirit is life and peace."
> (Romans 8:6)

There is truth to the old adage, *appearances can be deceiving.*

Some envision alcoholics as skid row bums, languishing on dirty city streets while downing liquor from a bottle wrapped in a brown paper bag. Statistics indicate only 3% of alcoholics fit this image.

Cathey's father always holds down a job and responsibly meets most of the family's financial needs. However, there is no doubt that his drinking diminishes his ability to fully function as a father and husband and negatively affects the entire family's emotional health.[6]

The number one obstacle for alcoholics and their families to receive healing from all forms and causes of dysfunction is denial. Unfortunately, a sense of shame and embarrassment in disclosing neediness prevents or delays enlisting the help and prayers of others—precisely what is necessary to no longer remain a dysfunctional family.

Scripture directs ...

**"Therefore confess your sins to each other and pray for each other so that you may be healed. The prayer of a righteous person is powerful and effective." (James 5:16)**

▶ **A dysfunctional family** is one in which improper and immature behavior of at least one parent damages the growth of individuality and the development of healthy relational skills among family members.

▶ **A dysfunctional family** is one in which family members are impaired emotionally, psychologically, and spiritually.

▶ **A dysfunctional family** is one in which all members are so emotionally and psychologically connected to one another that everyone is equally negatively impacted when only one family member experiences harm or encounters a problem.

Scripture warns about fostering dysfunction within one's family ...

**"Whoever brings ruin on their family
will inherit only wind, and the fool
will be servant to the wise."
(Proverbs 11:29)**

Cathey Brown longs for a functional family, where healthy interpersonal relationships are nurtured and where problems are addressed rather than avoided.

In order to cope and adapt, children of alcoholics will either draw attention to or away from themselves. As a child, Cathey strives to gain attention by performing seemingly perfectly in hopes that parental approval and her good behavior might distract from the preoccupation with alcohol. Children like Cathey also feel responsibility for the well-being of the family and focus on being problem fixers with the goal of becoming a functional family.[7]

Cathey knows now that she never had the resources to meet her family's desperate need, but there is One who is eager to give strength from His unlimited resources and to transform dysfunctional families into functional families.

> **"Look to the LORD and his strength;**
> **seek his face always."**
> **(1 Chronicles 16:11)**

## The Functional Family Is a Cultivating Family!

▶ **A functional family** is one in which proper and mature behavior of two parents cultivates a healthy balance between embracing *individuality* and embellishing *relational skills* among family members.

▶ **A functional family** is one in which healthy emotional, psychological, and spiritual growth is cultivated among family members.

▶ **A functional family** is one in which individual family members cultivate the ability to face problematic situations specific to them with personal confidence in God and self and with the general support of other family members.

Functional families cultivate confidence in God, which instills hope and confidence in children.

**"For you have been my hope,
Sovereign LORD,
my confidence since my youth."
(Psalm 71:5)**

When it comes to the various roles children play in order to cope, Cathey says the least likely to get help are the "heroes" like herself because they have the appearance of "having it all together." The achievements and the ensuing accolades fool people into thinking these children are emotionally healthy and do not need special attention.

"Scapegoats," on the other hand, are the *most* likely to get help because they purposely draw attention to themselves, frequently through negative behavior to divert attention away from major family problems. They are obviously troubled, thus special attention is directed their way to improve emotional health and to change behavior.[9]

The heart of God is to bring healing to every child and to deliver every family from debilitating dysfunction.

> **"He heals the brokenhearted
> and binds up their wounds."
> (Psalm 147:3)**

## Parents

▶ **The Dependent Parent**

The *overinvolved, possessive* parent is inconsistent and utilizes manipulative maneuvers to *control* children, along with additional forms of immature behavior to the detriment of other family members.

▶ **The Dictatorial Parent**

The *overcontrolling, inflexible* parent is performance-based and utilizes criticism to *condemn* children, along with additional forms of oppressive behavior to the detriment of other family members.

▶ **The Doting Parent**

The *overprotective, indulgent* parent is lacking in boundaries and utilizes rescuing to *cajole* children, along with additional forms of seemingly helpful behavior to the detriment of other family members.

▶ **The Demanding Parent**

The *overdirective, conformist* parent is overbearing and utilizes guilt and shame to *conform* children, along with additional forms of pressure-filled behavior to the detriment of other family members.

## CHILDREN

### ▶ The Responsible Child

The "*hero*" tries to fix the family problems and help create a positive family image with noteworthy achievement. This child receives positive attention but often develops perfectionistic, compulsive behaviors.

### ▶ The Rebellious Child

The "*scapegoat*" draws focus away from the family problems and onto their own personal problems by engaging in rebellious, uncontrollable behavior. This child consumes time and energy from the family members and often develops self-destructive life patterns.

### ▶ The Reclusive Child

The "*lost child*" hopes that by ignoring family problems, the difficulties will disappear. This child avoids attention and would like to just "fade into the woodwork." Reclusive children spend a lot of time alone and, therefore, are often lonely and withdrawn. They don't want to rock the boat.

### ▶ The Reveling Child

The "*mascot*" uses humor and antics to direct the focus away from family problems. This child is often hyperactive and usually seeks to be the center of attention.

## Role Reversal

▶ **Children** once did whatever they could to please their parents.

▶ **Parents** now do whatever they can to please their children.

However, the Bible says ...

> "Children, obey your parents in everything,
> for this pleases the Lord."
> (Colossians 3:20)

## Repeating Past Patterns

**QUESTION:** "I grew up in a messed up family, and I am now repeating many patterns from the past. What should I do?"

**ANSWER:** Ask the Lord to give you discernment in identifying which patterns need to be changed and wisdom in selecting several action steps that will enable you to move toward emotional health and healing. Tell those closest to you that you want to give up these unhealthy, childhood ways of thinking, reasoning, and acting from the past. Ask them to help hold you accountable.

> "When I was a child, I talked like a child,
> I thought like a child, I reasoned like a child.
> When I became a man, I put the ways of
> childhood behind me."
> (1 Corinthians 13:11)

## Define ACA

QUESTION: "What is meant by ACA?"

ANSWER: Children who grow up in homes with an alcoholic parent generally take on certain predictable and identifiable roles in the family in an effort to cope with the family's painful dysfunction. Unless efforts are extended to exchange these survival roles for functional healthy ways of dealing with family problems, children continue to play out these roles in adulthood, even after they have left their dysfunctional home environment. Although no longer children, because they still act the same way they acted as children, they are often referred to as ACA or ACOA, meaning "adult children of alcoholics."

"Brothers and sisters, stop thinking like children. In regard to evil be infants, but in your thinking be adults."
(1 Corinthians 14:20)

# CHARACTERISTICS

*The hero, the scapegoat, the lost child, and the clown.*

It is a curious phenomenon that, in case after case, children of alcoholics will assume various roles in order to cope with the stress of being raised by dysfunctional, chemically dependent parents. With Cathey Brown's bent toward performance and perfectionism, she describes herself as a "hero" during her childhood because she methodically is proactive in finding "fixes" for her dysfunctional family situation. Upon realizing she cannot control an out-of-control situation, guilt looms and an increased sense of personal deficiency burdens Cathey's spirit.[10]

The realization that child "heroes" do not have the power or resources to rescue dysfunctional families is punctuated in Cathey's life in 1981. Cathey's mother is admitted to the hospital for internal bleeding, half of her stomach is removed, and it's all related to excessive alcohol consumption.[11]

Scripture warns of the dangers and consequences of being consumed by alcohol: *"Who has woe? Who has sorrow? Who has strife? Who has complaints? Who has needless bruises? Who has bloodshot eyes? Those who linger over wine, who go to sample bowls of mixed wine. Do not gaze at wine when it is red, when it sparkles in the cup, when it goes down smoothly! In the end it bites like a snake and poisons like a viper"* (Proverbs 23:29–32).

As a grown-up, unresolved conflicts from Cathey's past lead her to the inconceivable—the very habits she fights so hard to avoid in childhood end up swallowing her up in adulthood.

If Cathey were taking the Checklist for Unresolved Conflicts, she undoubtedly would answer *yes* to almost every question, recognizing that the pain and heartache of being raised by dysfunctional, chemically dependent parents doesn't disappear upon turning 21.

A traumatic combination of circumstances—overachieving at work, a divorce, business challenges, and postpartum depression—draw Cathey first to chemical dependence on prescription drugs and then to alcohol to further numb herself from painful realities.[12]

Scripture teaches there is only one true source of peace in the midst of stressful circumstances, and it's found in the Lord of Peace.

> **"Now may the Lord of peace himself give you peace at all times and in every way."**
> **(2 Thessalonians 3:16)**

If you think you may have some unresolved conflicts from your past, complete the following checklist.

# Checklist for Unresolved Conflicts from Your Past

- ☐ Do you fear personal criticism?
- ☐ Do you give to others to the extent that it is harmful to you?
- ☐ Do you constantly seek approval?
- ☐ Do you suppress your emotions?
- ☐ Do you lie when you could easily tell the truth?
- ☐ Do you feel you must rescue others?
- ☐ Do you have difficulty having fun or relaxing?
- ☐ Do you confuse pity with love?
- ☐ Do you judge yourself too harshly?
- ☐ Do you find yourself easily manipulated?
- ☐ Do you assume too much responsibility?
- ☐ Do you have unresolved anger toward any family member?
- ☐ Do you avoid taking personal responsibility for your actions?
- ☐ Do you fear abandonment?
- ☐ Do you violate your own conscience in order to please others?
- ☐ Do you feel you need to control others?

**"Test me, LORD, and try me, examine my heart and my mind."
(Psalm 26:2)**

Rules exist in every area of life—in every part of the universe—whether written or spoken, known or unknown, established by God or by His creations. Rules reign and that is especially evident in dysfunctional families where they are rarely spoken and never written, but are abundantly clear. These rules wield absolute authority over the lives of those they govern.

Part of the problem with rules in dysfunctional families is that they are necessarily dysfunctional. They are established and reinforced by dysfunctional parents, instilled in vulnerable children, and disseminated throughout all their relationships. Dysfunctional patterns of behavior never remain in the family but spread out to every relationship.

No one is an island. Dysfunction can spread like a virus from person to person. Paul explained the connections in the family of God, the church, as having many parts yet forming one body.

**"Just as a body, though one, has many parts, but all its many parts form one body, so it is with Christ. For we were all baptized by one Spirit so as to form one body whether Jews or Gentiles, slave or free—and we were all given the one Spirit to drink. Even so the body is not made up of one part but of many. ... If one part suffers, every part suffers with it; if one part is honored, every part rejoices with it" (1 Cor. 12:12–14, 26).**

**Some of the rigid, damaging rules of dysfunctional families include ...**

▶ **Don't ever** appear weak, wrong, or less than perfect.

▶ **Don't ever** be spontaneously joyful or playful.

▶ **Don't ever** cause problems within the family.

▶ **Don't ever** directly address family issues, relationships, or problems.

▶ **Don't ever** divulge family secrets.

▶ **Don't ever** embarrass the family.

▶ **Don't ever** fail to fully support family members, no matter the circumstances.

▶ **Don't ever** make decisions independent of the family.

▶ **Don't ever** put anyone or anything above the family.

▶ **Don't ever** question or defy parental authority or family rules.

▶ **Don't ever** share personal needs, desires, or feelings.

▶ **Don't ever** speak badly about the family.

▶ **Don't ever** speak to an adult family member without first being spoken to.

▶ **Don't ever** talk about sex or other taboo subjects.

The Bible records both dysfunctional and functional adults following the ways of their parents and those of previous generations.

"He did evil in the eyes of the Lord, because he followed the ways of his father and mother and of Jeroboam son of Nebat, who caused Israel to sin. ...
In everything he followed the ways of his father Asa and did not stray from them; he did what was right in the eyes of the Lord."
(1 Kings 22:52, 43)

Dysfunctional family rules result in dysfunctional family members.

Besides producing the four types of roles children play in their homes, rigid destructive rules strike a devastating blow to the soul and spirit of impressionable little ones, twisting and distorting their perceptions of God, self, and others. While our heavenly Father put rules in place for our benefit to protect and produce good in us, dysfunctional family rules are for the benefit of those who set them and bring harm rather than hope to those in bondage to them.

Jesus valued the children brought to Him, while His own disciples sought to hinder them from receiving the good Christ had for them. Whether intentionally or not, dysfunctional parents today regard their children as the disciples did back then.

**"People were also bringing babies to Jesus for him to place his hands on them. When the disciples saw this, they rebuked them. But Jesus called the children to him and said, 'Let the little children come to me, and do not hinder them, for the kingdom of God belongs to such as these.'" (Luke 18:15–16)**

**Rigid dysfunctional rules damage family members to the point that they ...**

▶ **Don't engage** in open, honest communication—but demonstrate poor communication skills.

▶ **Don't develop** meaningful relationships—but establish enmeshed codependent relationships.

▶ **Don't express** personal feelings or opinions—but lack self-awareness.

▶ **Don't control** uncomfortable emotions—but experience emotional instability, depression, and anxiety.

▶ **Don't rationally** solve problems alone—but are prone to develop obsessions, compulsions, and addictions.

▶ **Don't feel** undesirable emotions without guilt and shame—but engage in self-injurious activities.

▶ **Don't tolerate** undesirable thoughts and feelings—but deny them both.

▶ **Don't experience** sexual desires without shame and guilt—but need to be in control or to be controlled.

▶ **Don't forgive** personal mistakes—but display perfectionist tendencies.

▶ **Don't separate** bad behavior from being bad—but harbor a deep fear of failure.

▶ **Don't develop** a positive self-image—but nurture a poor self-image and depend on others for a sense of self-worth.

▶ **Don't engage** in self-disclosure—but protect family secrets.

▶ **Don't value** and care for oneself emotionally or relationally—but accept an inordinate amount of mistreatment.

▶ **Don't set** appropriate boundaries with toxic people—but crave the approval of others.

▶ **Don't form** a separate identity from the family unit—but compete with and create divisions between family members.

▶ **Don't live** and enjoy a happy childhood—but feel emotionally empty and struggle with loneliness.

▶ **Don't assume** responsibility for personal contentment—but look for happiness in others.

▶ **Don't trust** God or people to provide love and security—but attempt to meet emotional needs in inappropriate ways.

Believing and accepting the truth about the depth, breadth, height, durability, and dependability of God's love is the greatest need of those who live with the damaging effects of rigid, dysfunctional family rules.

"For I am convinced that neither death nor
life, neither angels nor demons,
neither the present nor the future, nor
any powers, neither height nor depth, nor
anything else in all creation,
will be able to separate us from the love of
God that is in Christ Jesus our Lord."
(Romans 8:38–39)

Just as every individual family member is unique in a number of ways from other members, every family has some unique characteristics that set it apart from other families while at the same time continuing to share a host of similar attributes and qualities.

The Bible addresses the uniqueness of all God's creations from the perspective of a shepherd boy turned King ...

**"You created my inmost being; you knit me together in my mother's womb. I praise you because I am fearfully and wonderfully made; your works are wonderful, I know that full well." (Psalm 139:13–14)**

**Dysfunctional family systems are characterized by eight dominant traits.**

1. *Chaos*—drama and confusion reign with emotions ruling decision making. Reasoning and self-restraint take a backseat.

2. *Control*—keeping members in compliance with family rules and ideology is critical. Maintaining and supporting the hierarchy is essential to family preservation.

3. *Denial*—obvious family problems are unacknowledged, unaddressed, and unchanged. Lies are accepted as truth, and inappropriate behavior is often ignored.

4. *Inconsistency*—what was said one day is retracted the next. Expectations constantly change, and commitments are easily broken.

5. *Indifference*—emotional support of family members is blatantly lacking unless challenged by outsiders. Children are valued for their devotion and contribution to the family system.

6. *Instability*—emotions quickly fluctuate from happy to sad, pleased to angry. Change is constant and unforeseeable; insecurity runs rampant among family members.

7. *Shame*—members serve as emotional punching bags for each other, with shame being the most effective way of hurting, manipulating, and obtaining compliance.

8. *Unpredictability*—keeping each other guessing is everyone's long suit; therefore, what is allowed one day is forbidden the next day and what pleases someone today displeases them tomorrow.

Surely the Lord is the answer to the unmet needs that drive the maladaptive behavior of those who are members of dysfunctional families, those who are lonely of soul and spirit, those who feel isolated, disconnected, and emotionally empty.

**"Satisfy us in the morning with your unfailing love, that we may sing for joy and be glad all our days."**
**(Psalm 90:14)**

# CAUSES

Cathey Brown's journey into the throes of chemical addiction comes after her daughter, Catherine, is born.

A hormonal imbalance leads to anxiety, depression, and a loss of appetite. To remedy this condition, a doctor prescribes a powerful yet addictive drug and also recommends that Cathey drink two glasses of wine a day to relax her stomach muscles and encourage eating.[13] Cathey soon finds herself following in her parents' footsteps, focused on the gratification of the moment, not on the consequences of the future.

"I struggled with my addiction for a long time," Cathey recalls. "When I got into my own recovery, I learned about the problems that adult children of alcoholics have to deal with. I had grown up in that environment, and finally I had a label for it (ACA). But I suddenly realized that my daughter was at extremely high risk for repeating the same thing."[14]

Cathey longs to be set free and to prevent her daughter from being ensnared by chemical dependence.

Her experience is like that of the psalmist ...

**"When hard pressed, I cried to the LORD;
he brought me into a spacious place."
(Psalm 118:5)**

Cathey is familiar with chaotic families and the fact that many times holidays only exacerbate stress-filled environments.

As a child of alcoholics, Cathey remembers tension surrounding the annual dressing of the Christmas tree. "Putting up the Christmas tree was just an unbelievable event because Daddy had to have it perfect and so he would cut off limbs and drill holes and mother would get frustrated and leave the room. We'd get tinsel on the floor and that was a mess. It was just not a joyous occasion."[16]

Growing up, Cathey realizes that the media images portraying the wonders of Christmas—angelic faces glowing with the gaiety of the holiday season—are not her reality, and her memories haunt her into adulthood and impact her marriage. Cathey recalls becoming belligerent and depressed prior to Christmas, not showing up for family events and even trying to pick fights with her husband and daughter. Fearing disappointment and failure, she becomes a self-saboteur of sorts, dismantling beforehand what she believes will bring her pain in the long run.

Years later, Cathey has gained insight concerning the motivation behind her actions. "Part of it was just being comfortable that I was worthy of people doing things for me, that I was lovable, that I deserved the center of attention." Cathey adds that she has since learned that it isn't about "deserving" special attention, but just letting her family love her for who she is.[17]

The love of Cathey's family mirrors the depth of the love of God ...

"The Lord, the Lord, the compassionate and gracious God, slow to anger, abounding in love and faithfulness, maintaining love to thousands, and forgiving wickedness, rebellion and sin. Yet he does not leave the guilty unpunished; he punishes the children and their children for the sin of the parents to the third and fourth generation." (Exodus 34:6–7)

The truth of Exodus chapter 34 is clearly seen in the fact that the sinful behavior of parents is more often than not passed on to children through the natural process of simulation—of replicating what they experience. Something cannot come from nothing. Problem behavior does not come from nowhere but often from a home where problem behavior is practiced by adults and picked up by children.

Most of us do not exhibit bad behavior because we want to do bad things, but because we have deep-seated inner problems that drive and manifest themselves in outward bad behavior.

If you want to change how you act, first change your heart. Jesus said it this way ...

**"It is from within, out of a person's heart, that evil thoughts come —sexual immorality, theft, murder, adultery, greed, malice, deceit, lewdness, envy, slander, arrogance and folly. All these evils come from inside and defile a person." (Mark 7:21–23)**

With youngsters more is caught than taught. Without intervention brought on by a changed heart resulting in changed behavior, dysfunctional behavior will continue to beget dysfunctional behavior.

## Dysfunctional Families Produce Dysfunctional Families

▶ **The Chaotic Family**

- Both household and individuals are poorly organized.
- Family is plagued by problems.
- Parents are inconsistent and indecisive.
- Children are emotionally abandoned.

**RESULT**

Family members are not connected.

**REMEDY**

"... *a ruler with discernment and knowledge maintains order*" (Proverbs 28:2).

## ▶ The Controlling Family

- Structure is overly rigid.
- Tone is authoritative and dictatorial.
- Parents tend to be faultfinding and critical.
- Children are task oriented; value is placed on their performance.

### RESULT

Family members are fearful and insensitive.

### REMEDY

*"Fathers, do not exasperate your children; instead, bring them up in the training and instruction of the Lord"* (Ephesians 6:4).

## ▶ The Coddling Family

- Parental authority is lacking.
- Feelings are overprotected.
- Disagreements are avoided.
- Children are the center of attention.

### RESULT

Family members are undisciplined.

### REMEDY

*"... correction and instruction are the way to life"* (Proverbs 6:23).

## ▶ The Codependent Family

- Conformity is strong within the family.
- Self-direction is lacking.
- Parents are overly possessive.
- Children are smothered.

### RESULT

Family members are insecure.

### REMEDY

*"Love the LORD your God with all your heart and with all your soul and with all your strength"* (Deuteronomy 6:5).

After being raised in a dysfunctional family by alcoholics and later becoming an alcoholic herself, Cathey shares profound and encouraging insights for those struggling down her same path toward a functional family style: "Recovery is a process. It is not an event."[18]

As Cathey seeks help for her addictions and takes steps toward creating a cultivating family, she is increasingly concerned for her daughter, who could repeat generational patterns of alcoholism:

> "I discovered a lot of kids like my daughter, kids who needed some type of support group, some type of education, some type of outlet for talking about what was going on in their families, but there was nothing for them. They needed a different way to cope with their background than I had. Somebody needed to teach them that their feelings were okay, and rather than act out or push themselves to the limit as I had done, they could learn how to cope with it."[19]

To one day be part of a functional, cultivating family the fears and needs of children of alcoholics must be addressed in the recovery process.

Ministering to children is close to the heart of God ...

**"'Truly I tell you, anyone who will not receive the kingdom of God like a little child will never enter it.' And he took the children in his arms, placed his hands on them and blessed them."**
**(Mark 10:15–16)**

▶ **The Cultivating Family**

- Structure and discipline are maintained by parents.
- Individual responsibility is required.
- Love and obedience to God are developed.
- Children are secure.

**RESULT**

Family relationships are balanced.

**REMEDY**

*"There, in the presence of the LORD your God, you and your families shall eat and shall rejoice in everything you have put your hand to, because the LORD your God has blessed you"* (Deuteronomy 12:7).

Since family dysfunction is generally passed down from one generation to the next, determining the point of the dysfunction's origin may be impossible for many families. Whatever provided the impetus for the deterioration of family interaction was likely a traumatic event that so altered the fabric of the family that its members were unable to recover normalcy and succumbed to dysfunction.

The same process can be seen in an individual who undergoes a trauma so impactful it changes the course of the person's life. The individual's perceptions of God, self, others, and life as a whole are dramatically altered, so much so, that the person seems to have become "another person" and might even be seen by family members and close friends as now being a "stranger" to them.

Unless such life-altering events are examined, processed, and dealt with in a healthy way from a balanced, biblical perspective, healthy normalcy will be lost and a new unhealthy normalcy will give birth to a dysfunctional lifestyle.

The good news is that the opposite is equally true. A traumatic experience has the potential to turn a dysfunctional person into a positive, productive individual. Such was the case with a Hebrew scholar named Saul.

*"I too was convinced that I ought to do all that was possible to oppose the name of Jesus of Nazareth. ... About noon, King Agrippa, as I was on the road, I saw a light from heaven, brighter than the sun, blazing around me and my companions. We all fell to the ground, and I heard a voice saying to me in Aramaic, 'Saul, Saul, why do you persecute me? It is hard for you to kick against the goads.' Then I asked, 'Who are you, Lord?' 'I am Jesus, whom you are persecuting,' the Lord replied. 'Now get up and stand on your feet. I have appeared to you to appoint you as a servant and as a witness of what you have seen and will see of me.' ... So then, King Agrippa, I was not disobedient to the vision from heaven"* (Acts 26:9, 13–16, 19).

Just as there can be multiple reasons people do the things they do, there can be a multitude of reasons for a family being dysfunctional. For some families the ...

▶ **Presence** of chemical addiction results in maladaptive behavior.

▶ **Existence** of emotional, physical, or psychological disturbances damages family members.

▶ **Tolerance** of abusive behavior within the family prevents healthy interaction.

▶ **Adherence** to a rigid, dogmatic belief system leads to bondage.

▶ **Unexpected** death of a significant family member creates a crisis of faith that causes chaos.

Whatever dynamic exists within a family that results in dysfunction, the Lord is able to intervene and bring His life-changing truths into that family to transform it into a healthy, functional family through which He can work to transform other families to His praise and glory.

**"Now the Lord is the Spirit, and where the Spirit of the Lord is, there is freedom. And we all, who with unveiled faces contemplate the Lord's glory, are being transformed into his image with ever-increasing glory, which comes from the Lord, who is the Spirit." (2 Corinthians 3:17–18)**

Cathey is determined to bring dysfunction to a dead end with her family.

Besides amply providing love and a sense of significance to her daughter, Cathey strives to create a secure environment where Catherine feels free to express her feelings concerning her needs and her family's struggles. This is atypical for children of alcoholics, where the unspoken message is "we're not going to talk about it."

Cathey recalls a specific incident where Catherine, as a teenager, freely expresses her feelings through standing by a decision she has made. With a business trip scheduled to California the same weekend as Catherine's birthday, Cathey had hoped her daughter would join her so they could celebrate together. Catherine doesn't warm to the idea, she prefers to stay home and celebrate with friends. Cathey is gravely disappointed, and admittedly pines: "But I'm the one that gave birth to you and I want to spend this time with you."[20]

Catherine isn't swayed, and maturely responds: "Well, Mom I love you and I'm really not saying this to hurt your feelings, but you're really not going to make me feel guilty about it."[21]

Cathey's disappointment quickly dissipates as she recognizes her daughter's emotional strength and her healthy ability to express her needs and not buckle under to others' wishes or demands. Love, significance, and security; helping to meet these needs among family members is a sure way to drive away dysfunction.

Scripture encourages as we allow God to minister through us ...

**"And let us consider how we may spur one another on toward love and good deeds."**
**(Hebrews 10:24)**

## Three God-Given Inner Needs

In reality, we have all been created with three God-given inner needs: the needs for love, significance, and security.[22]

▶ **Love**—to know that someone is unconditionally committed to our best interest

*"My command is this: Love each other as I have loved you"* (John 15:12).

▶ **Significance**—to know that our lives have meaning and purpose

*"I cry out to God Most High, to God who fulfills his purpose for me"* (Psalm 57:2 ESV).

▶ **Security**—to feel accepted and a sense of belonging

*"Whoever fears the Lord has a secure fortress, and for their children it will be a refuge"* (Proverbs 14:26).

## The Ultimate Need-Meeter

**"Why did God give us these deep inner needs, knowing that people and self-effort fail us?"**

God gave us these inner needs so that we would come to know Him as our Need-Meeter. Our needs are designed by God to draw us into a deeper dependence on Christ. God did not create any person or position or any amount of power or possessions to meet the deepest needs in our lives. If a person or thing could meet all our needs, we wouldn't need God! The Lord will use circumstances and bring positive people into our lives as an extension of His care and compassion, but ultimately only God can satisfy all the needs of our hearts. The Bible says ...

> **"The Lord will guide you always;**
> **he will satisfy your needs in a sun-scorched**
> **land and will strengthen your frame.**
> **You will be like a well-watered garden,**
> **like a spring whose waters never fail."**
> **(Isaiah 58:11)**

The apostle Paul revealed this truth by first asking, *"What a wretched man I am. Who will rescue me from this body that is subject to death?"* He then answers his own question by saying he is saved by *"Jesus Christ our Lord!"* (Romans 7:24–25).

All along, the Lord planned to meet our deepest needs for ...

▶ **Love**—*"I* [the Lord] *have loved you with an everlasting love; I have drawn you with unfailing kindness"* (Jeremiah 31:3).

▶ **Significance**—*"'For I know the plans I have for you,' declares the* LORD*, 'plans to prosper you and not to harm you, plans to give you hope and a future'"* (Jeremiah 29:11).

▶ **Security**—*"The* LORD *himself goes before you and will be with you; he will never leave you nor forsake you. Do not be afraid; do not be discouraged"* (Deuteronomy 31:8).

The truth is that our God-given needs for love, significance, and security can be legitimately met in Christ Jesus! Philippians 4:19 makes it plain ...

**"My God will meet all your needs according to the riches of his glory in Christ Jesus."**

## ▶ WRONG BELIEF

"My parents did not give me the unconditional love, significance, and security I needed as a child. Since my past is unchangeable, I can't change who I am today."

### RIGHT BELIEF

"My need for unconditional love, significance, and security is being met by Christ, who lives in me. Although I can't change my past, I can change my attitude about my past. I will depend on God to empower me to learn healthy ways of relating to my family."

**"Bear with each other and forgive one another if any of you has a grievance against someone. Forgive as the Lord forgave you." (Colossians 3:13)**

An authentic relationship with Christ is never characterized by dysfunction. His love for you is unfailing and unconditional and is always focused on your highest good. He longs to walk with you through life day by day, moment by moment, all the while working to complete what He has begun in those who belong to Him—transformation into His likeness. Learning how to think like Him, speak like Him, and act like Him is what transformation is all about.

Your deepest needs for love, significance, and security can be met only in Christ. Depending on others alone leads only to dysfunction. He is inviting you today into an authentic relationship, but first there are four spiritual truths you need to know.

### FOUR POINTS OF GOD'S PLAN

#### #1 God's Purpose for You is *Salvation.*

What was God's motivation in sending Jesus Christ to earth?

To express His love for you by saving you!

The Bible says, *"God so loved the world that he gave his one and only Son, that whoever believes in him shall not perish but have eternal life. For God did not send his Son into the world to condemn the world, but to save the world through him"* (John 3:16–17).

What was Jesus' purpose in coming to earth?

To forgive your sins, to empower you to have victory over sin, and to enable you to live a fulfilled life!

Jesus said, *"I have come that they may have life, and that they may have it more abundantly"* (John 10:10 NKJV).

### #2 Your Problem is *Sin*.

What exactly is sin?

Sin is living independently of God's standard—knowing what is right, but choosing what is wrong.

The Bible says, *"If anyone, then, knows the good they ought to do and doesn't do it, it is sin for them"* (James 4:17).

What is the major consequence of sin?

Spiritual death, eternal separation from God.

Scripture states, *"Your iniquities* [sins] *have separated you from your God"* (Isaiah 59:2).

*"The wages of sin is death, but the gift of God is eternal life in Christ Jesus our Lord"* (Romans 6:23).

### #3 God's Provision for You is the *Savior*.

Can anything remove the penalty for sin?

Yes! Jesus died on the cross to personally pay the penalty for your sins.

The Bible says, *"God demonstrates his own love for us in this: While we were still sinners, Christ died for us"* (Romans 5:8).

What is the solution to being separated from God?

Belief in (entrusting your life to) Jesus Christ as the only way to God the Father.

Jesus says, *"I am the way and the truth and the life. No one comes to the Father except through me"* (John 14:6).

*"Believe in the Lord Jesus, and you will be saved"* (Acts 16:31).

### #4 Your Part is *Surrender.*

Give Christ control of your life, entrusting yourself to Him.

*"Jesus said to his disciples, 'Whoever wants to be my disciple must deny themselves and take up their cross* [die to your own self-rule] *and follow me. For whoever wants to save their life will lose it, but whoever loses their life for me will find it. What good will it be for someone to gain the whole world, yet forfeit their soul?'"* (Matthew 16:24–26).

Place your faith in (rely on) Jesus Christ as your personal Lord and Savior and reject your "good works" as a means of earning God's approval.

*"It is by grace you have been saved, through faith— and this is not from yourselves, it is the gift of God—not by works, so that no one can boast"* (Ephesians 2:8–9).

The moment you choose to receive Jesus as your Lord and Savior—entrusting your life to Him—He comes to live inside you. Then He gives you His power to live the fulfilled life God has planned for you.

If you want to be fully forgiven by God and become the person God created you to be, you can tell Him in a simple, heartfelt prayer like this:

## PRAYER OF SALVATION

*"God, I want a real relationship with You.
I admit that many times I've chosen to go
my own way instead of Your way.
Please forgive me for my sins.
Jesus, thank You for dying on the cross to
pay the penalty for my sins.
Come into my life to be
my Lord and my Savior.
Change me from the inside out
and make me the person
You created me to be.
In Your holy name I pray. Amen."*

## What Can You Now Expect?

**If you sincerely prayed this prayer, look at what God says!**

"His divine power has given us
everything we need for a godly life
through our knowledge of him who called us
by his own glory and goodness.
Through these he has given us his
very great and precious promises,
so that through them you may participate
in the divine nature,
having escaped the corruption
in the world caused by evil desires."
(2 Peter 1:3–4)

# STEPS TO SOLUTION

The year 1981 proves to be a pivotal one for Cathey Brown. Not only does her mother experience the traumatic stomach surgery traced directly to excessive alcohol consumption, but her doctor looks Cathey squarely in the eye and admonishes: "If you continue to drink, in 10 years you'll be where your mother is now."[23]

A second sobering wake-up call comes while watching a television program featuring former First Lady Betty Ford's struggles with alcohol and the anticipated opening of the Betty Ford Center. "I began to think for the first time that if a former First Lady could have this problem and be so public about it, that maybe I wasn't so bad, maybe I could do something about my problem."[24]

But Cathey soon learns that not only can she not do "something" about her problem, she can't do "anything" about it. Rather, she must desperately rely on the help of Someone else.

> **"I lift up my eyes to the mountains—**
> **where does my help come from?**
> **My help comes from the LORD,**
> **the Maker of heaven and earth."**
> **(Psalm 121:1–2)**

Cathey discovers the truth and the truth eventually sets her free. It is a sweet surrender, experienced only after acknowledging that in her own strength she can not defeat the dysfunction spawned by generational patterns of alcoholism.

"I tried to study my way out of it," Cathey muses. "I tried to rationalize my way out of it. I tried to bargain my way out of it. But finally, one day when I was in my office by myself, I just got down on my knees and cried my heart out: 'God, I can't do this! You have to do it, and I don't know what else to do except turn it over to you.' The next morning I woke up—I'll never forget the date, April 17, 1981—and I just had this feeling in my heart that I wasn't going to drink anymore."[25]

## KEY VERSE TO MEMORIZE

*"If you hold to my teaching,
you are really my disciples.
Then you will know the truth,
and the truth will set you free."*
(John 8:31–32)

## Key Passage to Read

### BREAKING FREE OF FAMILY FAILURES

Five chapters in the book of Genesis record the account of how God uses one son of a dysfunctional family to dramatically and forever change, not just one, but 11 dysfunctional families. Joseph's story in Genesis is a biblical portrait of what God can do in dysfunctional family relationships when one family member is yielded to God.

### JOSEPH'S DYSFUNCTIONAL FAMILY
### GENESIS 37

Joseph is the eleventh son of Jacob, born in his old age, born by the wife he adored. Jacob loves Joseph more than any of his other older sons. When Joseph's older brothers see their father *favoring* him over them, they seethe with *jealousy* and *anger*. In their vengeance they sell Joseph into slavery. Clearly, their family exhibits ...

- Poor communication
- Partiality
- Jealousy
- Dishonesty
- Anger
- Vengefulness
- Disloyalty
- Bitterness

## JOSEPH'S WALK WITH THE LORD
## GENESIS 39, 41

In spite of the mistreatment Joseph received at the hands of his angry brothers, he refused to allow their betrayal to make him an angry and bitter man. Instead, he chose by an act of his will to remain ...

- Yielded to God's ways
- Obedient to authority
- Trustworthy
- Morally pure
- Faithful
- Honest
- Humble
- Consistent

## JOSEPH'S RESPONSE TO HIS FAMILY
## GENESIS 42

When Joseph was reunited with his brothers through the providence of God, he harbored no desire for revenge, no compulsion to get even, no attempt to do them harm. Again, by an act of his will, he chose to be ...

- Giving
- Forgiving
- Honoring

## Joseph's Response to God
## Genesis 50

At the death of their father, Joseph's older brothers again feared he would pay them back for all the wrongs they had done to him. But Joseph chose to focus not on the harm they had intended for him, but on the good God intended for them all. Thus Joseph's attitude toward God was ...

- Willing
- Persevering
- Faithful

## Don't Be a Prisoner of Your Past!

Like Joseph, choose to have God's mind-set toward those who have injured you.

> **"You intended to harm me,
> but God intended it for good."
> (Genesis 50:20)**

There is an adage in Christian ministry—God can use your "mess" to become your message, and He can use your "test" to become your testimony. That is certainly Cathey Brown's experience, drawing from her own personal pain to devote herself to helping transform the lives of others. Cathey has reached the target thousands upon thousands of times, establishing through Rainbow Days a curriculum-based support group program for counseling the dysfunctional children of alcoholics.

Cathey remembers a precious moment when she was leading a group and a seven-year-old girl comes running toward her exclaiming, "Cathey, Cathey guess what!" Cathey appropriately responds, "What?" The little girl recounts that her father is an alcoholic and her mother divorced him, then married another man who also is an alcoholic, but the little girl's mood continues to be remarkably upbeat. "Well, guess what," she continues most assuredly, "when I grow up I don't have to marry an alcoholic."[26]

God's Word assures us that through the good times and the bad, God is unfolding a perfect plan ...

**"And we know that in all things
God works for the good of those
who love him, who have been called
according to his purpose."
(Romans 8:28)**

# Reaching the Target: Transformation!

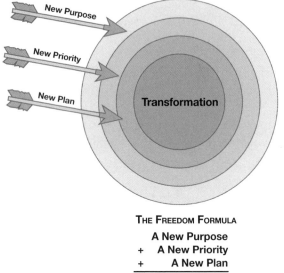

THE FREEDOM FORMULA

A New Purpose
+ A New Priority
+ A New Plan
_____
A Transformed Life

## My Personalized Plan

Life is a series of choices! I cannot embrace the functional freedom God has planned for me until I make the choice to release the hold dysfunction has on me. My life cannot be filled with the positive blessings of functionality until I choose to empty it of the negative practices of dysfunctionality. My heart cannot be filled with the hope of functionality until I choose to empty it of the despair of dysfunctionality.

If I choose to put away the past and embrace the future, then I will have to choose to take my God by the hand and walk through the following steps with Him.

### HOW TO PUT AWAY THE PAST[27]

I will ...

▶ **Give myself time to grieve the past.**[28]

- Pray for God to reveal my grief.
- Choose to be honest about my pain.
- Give myself permission to grieve.
- List all my painful experiences and then write the word "past" by each one.

*"Very truly I tell you, you will weep and mourn while the world rejoices. You will grieve, but your grief will turn to joy"* (John 16:20).

### ▶ Give up my need to be controlling.

- Recognize that God has ultimate control.
- Trust in God's sovereign rule over my relationships.
- Submit to God's control of my personal life.
- Rest in God's love and care for me.

*"Cast your cares on the LORD and he will sustain you; he will never let the righteous be shaken"* (Psalm 55:22).

### ▶ Give Christ first place in my heart.

- Ask Jesus to be Lord of my life.
- Accept His forgiveness and love.
- Be aware of His constant presence within me.
- Allow Him to lead in all I say and do.

*"Whoever wants to be my disciple must deny themselves and take up their cross daily and follow me. For whoever wants to save their life will lose it, but whoever loses their life for me will save it"* (Luke 9:23–24).

### ▶ Give God thanks for my past.

- Know that God will be faithful to heal me.
- Recognize that difficult relationships mature me.
- Look for positive ways God can use the pain in my life.
- Focus on developing the character of Christ within me.

*"Give thanks in all circumstances; for this is God's will for you in Christ Jesus"* (1 Thessalonians 5:18).

▶ **Give attention to how I responded to my circumstances as a child.**

Was I ...

- The responsible child?
- The rebellious child?
- The reclusive child?
- The reveling child?

*"The heart of the discerning acquires knowledge, for the ears of the wise seek it out"* (Proverbs 18:15).

▶ **Give thought to my present dysfunctional characteristics.**

- Pray for God to reveal my weaknesses.
- Pray for wisdom to understand how to change.
- Pray that I will draw on Christ, who is my strength, to make changes.
- Pray for wise and discerning friends to enlighten and encourage me.

*"Search me, God, and know my heart; test me and know my anxious thoughts. See if there is any offensive way in me, and lead me in the way everlasting"* (Psalm 139:23–24).

▶ **Give consideration to my God-given rights.**

- I have the right to obey God rather than others.
- I have the right to a clear conscience.
- I have the right to follow the Word of God.
- I have the right to live in my God-appointed role.

*"We must obey God rather than human beings!"* (Acts 5:29).

▶ **Give myself boundaries.**[29]

- Define who I am: "I am a child of God," and who I am not: "I am not a piece of property."
- Refuse to be manipulated or mistreated and learn to say, "No."
- Stop playing the victim: "As an adult, I am not powerless."
- Stop blaming others and do not seek their approval: "I'll take responsibility for my own behavior."

*"Am I now trying to win the approval of human beings, or of God? Or am I trying to please people? If I were still trying to please people, I would not be a servant of Christ"* (Galatians 1:10).

▶ **Give up resentment.**

- Consider the consequences of unforgiveness.
- Confess my own areas of unforgiveness.
- Contemplate the sins for which I have received forgiveness.
- Choose to forgive and keep on choosing to forgive.

*"Be kind and compassionate to one another, forgiving each other, just as in Christ God forgave you"* (Ephesians 4:32).

▶ **Give time to restoring healthy family relationships.**

- Be the one to begin rebuilding relationships.
- Be willing to spend quality time in order to develop healthy relationships.
- Be generous with grace toward others whose attitudes and actions are negative.
- Be a channel of God's unconditional love and acceptance to others.

*"If you are offering your gift at the altar and there remember that your brother or sister has something against you, leave your gift there in front of the altar. First go and be reconciled to them; then come and offer your gift"* (Matthew 5:23–24).

If you were raised in a dysfunctional family, you likely never learned how to take care of yourself but only how to take care of others and how to manipulate others to take care of you in return. In order to move from dysfunction to functioning as a healthy adult, it is imperative that you switch from being dependent on others to being *actively dependent* on God to meet your needs. That means you will enter into a partnership with God in which you will work together with Him toward attaining maturity, which will result in your learning contentment and experiencing fulfillment.

**"I know what it is to be in need,
and I know what it is to have plenty.
I have learned the secret of being content in any and every situation, whether well fed or hungry, whether living in plenty or in want."
(Philippians 4:12)**

As you practice depending on God through developing a deepening relationship with Him, cooperate with Him by doing your part in assuming some responsibilities for yourself.

▶ **Claim** your identity in Christ as a worthwhile person, one for whom He died and now lives within.

▶ **Learn** to identify your needs and wants by asking God for insight and by understanding your basic needs for love, significance, and security.

▶ **Make** the effort every day to do something to help meet your needs, such as reading Scriptures that emphasis your significance to God, having a meaningful conversation with a friend, or doing a good deed for someone.

▶ **Realize** feelings are merely feelings. It is how you express them that is right or wrong

▶ **Allow** yourself to have painful feelings. Remind yourself that feelings are not fatal no matter how much you may hurt inside from wrongs done to you or expectations that are not met.

▶ **Welcome** pleasant feelings, hold on to them, and relish in them.

▶ **Look** for things to do and people to be with that make you laugh.

▶ **Improve** your self-image by learning a new skill, taking a class, or improving your personal appearance.

▶ **Spend** time and money on yourself by reading a favorite book, buying something you like, or doing something you enjoy.

▶ **Feel** good about your accomplishments at work, at home, at church, and in relationships.

▶ **Begin** prioritizing significant people and meaningful activities and learn to say *no* to all that would keep you from saying *yes* to God.

▶ **Practice** telling others that you care about them but that you are responsible to God to care for yourself as well: "I really do care about you and would like to be with you, but I have some responsibilities I must take care of. Neglecting them would be bad for me and displeasing to God. Let's plan something else another time."

▶ **Stop** seeking to control others or allowing them to control you but rather, seek freedom in your relationships.

▶ **Guard** against engaging in obsessions or compulsive behaviors by being aware of your thoughts and actions. Illicit the help of others to remind you and hold you accountable.

▶ **Take** time to focus on God's love for you and learn to see yourself as He sees you by completing the 31-day devotional *Seeing Yourself Through God's Eyes*. Memorize Scriptures that speak of His love for you.

"For those who are led by the Spirit of God are the children of God.
The Spirit you received does not make you slaves, so that you live in fear again;
rather, the Spirit you received brought about your adoption to sonship.
And by him we cry, 'Abba, Father.'
The Spirit himself testifies with our spirit that we are God's children.
Now if we are children, then we are heirs—heirs of God and co-heirs with Christ,
if indeed we share in his sufferings in order that we may also share in his glory."
(Romans 8:14-17)

If the way to eat an elephant is one bite at a time, the way to change a family is by changing one member at a time, and that member is you—the only one you *can* change. Given the enmeshed system of a dysfunctional family, just one member can rock the boat enough to create a tidal wave. The key is knowing whether to rock the boat or get out of it.

It takes enormous courage and determination to try to become functional while maintaining close ties with a dysfunctional family of origin. The ties that bind the members together can choke the life out of one who seeks to struggle against them in an attempt to become free of them. For many, freedom can come only when distance creates a loosening of the cords so that there is room for movement.

If you desire to truly walk in the freedom Christ purchased for you, you will have no choice but to cut the cords that hold you and every member of your family in bondage to one another. It is impossible to find your true identity in Christ while remaining bound to a family system that is based on owning you and providing your identity for you.

God's Word is clear ...

**"You shall have no other gods before me."**
**(Exodus 20:3)**

▶ **As you seek to make Christ your rightful owner ... Acknowledge** the dysfunction within your family and particularly your own personal dysfunction.

▶ **Admit** to God, yourself, and at least one other trustworthy, functional person that you have a problem.

▶ **Don't** attempt to change anyone but yourself, the only person you *can* change.

▶ **Believe** that you can change with the power of God working in and through you.

▶ **Memorize** and repeat Psalm 25:15: *"My eyes are ever on the LORD, for only he will release my feet from the snare."*

▶ **Refuse** to take on the responsibilities for other family members.

▶ **Focus** on your own feelings, coping mechanisms, and the role(s) you play within your family.

▶ **Construct** positive, biblical roles of your own choosing for your life now.

▶ **Look** at your own character defects.

▶ **Determine** what you can do to improve your life.

▶ **Identify** and list behaviors that enable the dysfunction to continue.

▶ **Join** a 12-step program or other support group if appropriate.

**As you seek to change, use these questions for personal reflection and to gain insight.**

▶ **What** took place in your family as you were growing up?

▶ **What** roles did you take on? How did they affect you then, and how are they effecting you now?

▶ **What** messages about yourself did you get from your family?

▶ **What** beliefs did you form about yourself then? About God? About life? About your family?

▶ **What** beliefs do you have about yourself today? About God? About life? About your family?

▶ **What** is the basis for the beliefs you have today?

▶ **Does** it feel good or bad to be a member of your family today?

▶ **How** do you feel when you are around your family? Happy? Sad? Angry? Depressed? Shameful? Guilty?

▶ **Do** you feel like a little child or a victim again, or do you feel like an adult?

▶ **Do** you assume any childhood role when you are around your family now?

▶ **Did** you have anger issues as a child? Do you have them now?

▶ **When** and why did you start to feel as you do?

▶ **As** an adult, did you switch your role from being a victim to being an abuser or an addict?

▶ **Do** these questions stir up feelings in you that reflect current problems in your life or past problems from your family of origin?

It is important that you share both your past and current feelings of anger and pain with a safe and mature person who can help you process them and release them and your family to God. In releasing them to God, you will find that He will release you and set you free.

> "I will keep you and will make you
> to be a covenant for the people
> and a light for the Gentiles,
> to open eyes that are blind,
> to free captives from prison and
> to release from the dungeon those
> who sit in darkness."
> (Isaiah 42:6–7)

Cultivating your family for the future involves sowing seeds of unity, but Cathey knows authentic healing must begin with one collective, "tilling the dirt," act—*forgiveness.*

Cathey finds true freedom from her past through forgiveness: forgiving her parents for withholding a nurturing childhood, forgiving her dad for his abuse, and forgiving herself for her own sins and shortcomings. And what has blossomed for Cathey as a result of deliberately choosing to forgive is a fresh, new way to love her parents and to receive their love.[31]

Forgiveness is more often than not the starting point for restoring relationships, and it is critical for cultivating emotionally and spiritually healthy families.

The Bible reiterates our need to forgive time and time again, even endlessly, according to the following Scriptures ...

**"Then Peter came to Jesus and asked, 'Lord, how many times shall I forgive my brother or sister who sins against me? Up to seven times?' Jesus answered, 'I tell you, not seven times, but seventy-seven times.'" (Matthew 18:21–22)**

**As you endeavor to cultivate the hearts of family members …**

▶ **Emphasize** the uniqueness of each individual family member.

- Observe family members and identify two or three positive actions, attitudes, or other attributes that distinguish each one from the others.

- Find an opportunity to compliment each relative in private, express your pride in them for exhibiting Christlike qualities and your appreciation of their individual uniqueness and positive example.

*"Even so the body is not made up of one part but of many. Now if the foot should say, 'Because I am not a hand, I do not belong to the body,' it would not for that reason stop being part of the body. And if the ear should say, 'Because I am not an eye, I do not belong to the body,' it would not for that reason stop being part of the body. If the whole body were an eye, where would the sense of hearing be? If the whole body were an ear, where would the sense of smell be?"* (1 Corinthians 12:14–17).

▶ **Seek** togetherness, but also encourage individuality.[32]

- Plan some family projects that will utilize the strengths and skills of each individual family member.

- Have regularly scheduled family meetings, and at least one time a month celebrate individual accomplishments of family members.

*"There are different kinds of gifts, but the same Spirit distributes them. There are different kinds of service, but the same Lord. There are different kinds of working, but in all of them and in everyone it is the same God at work. Now to each one the manifestation of the Spirit is given for the common good"* (1 Corinthians 12:4–7).

▶ **Maintain** consistency in the messages you communicate.

- Practice what you preach by making sure you don't have one standard for family members and quite another for yourself, or commend certain behavior one day and condemn it the next.

- Do what you say you will do regarding discipline and unbiased administering of rewards and repercussions toward family members.

*"Out of the same mouth come praise and cursing. My brothers and sisters, this should not be. Can both fresh water and salt water flow from the same spring? My brothers and sisters, can a fig tree bear olives, or a grapevine bear figs? Neither can a salt spring produce fresh water. Who is wise and understanding among you? Let them show it by their good life, by deeds done in the humility that comes from wisdom"* (James 3:10–13).

▶ **Practice** immediate but appropriate discipline.

- Establish and administer rewards and repercussions that fit the particular behavior so family members will consider you fair and just.

- Don't make idle threats but state what will happen when certain actions are taken by family members. Then follow through when you are alone with an offender, explaining that choosing a behavior includes choosing the reward or repercussion associated with the behavior; therefore, you are honoring the person's choice.

*"Whoever spares the rod hates their children, but the one who loves their children is careful to discipline them"* (Proverbs 13:24).

▶ **Allow** a generous margin for mistakes.

- For the most part disobedience is intentional, whereas mistakes are unintentional and are based on miscommunication, misinformation, or poor judgment. Give people the benefit of the doubt and then clarify instructions and agreements.

- Do not expect perfection from family members but request they aim for excellence by doing the best they can to comply with family agreements and expectations.

*"Be kind and compassionate to one another, forgiving each other, just as in Christ God forgave you"* (Ephesians 4:32).

▶ **Encourage** the appropriate expression of feelings.

- Affirm the feelings of family members by acknowledging them and allowing the appropriate expression of them.

- Encourage the healthy expression of feelings that are natural and warranted as a result of sad, difficult, unfair, or hurtful circumstances.

*"The purposes of a person's heart are deep waters, but one who has insight draws them out"* (Proverbs 20:5).

▶ **Promote** and develop natural talents and abilities.

- Take note of the individual talents and abilities of family members. Provide opportunities for them to be developed inside and outside the family.
- Engage the family in various athletic, cultural, and social activities that will expose and enhance individual talents and abilities.

*"Start children off on the way they should go, and even when they are old they will not turn from it"* (Proverbs 22:6).

▶ **Require** family members to take responsibility for their own attitudes and actions.

- Do not blame others for your choices, and do not allow members of the family to shirk responsibility for their individual attitudes and actions by trying to blame someone else for their choices.
- Empower family members by impressing on them their individual freedom to think, make decisions, and act for themselves, which makes them personally responsible for the choices they make

*"Each one should test their own actions. Then they can take pride in themselves alone, without comparing themselves to someone else, for each one should carry their own load"* (Galatians 6:4–5).

▶ **Treat** everyone with love and respect.

- Apply Jesus' words: *"Do to others as you would have them do to you"* (Luke 6:31).
- Read 1 Corinthians chapter 13 and make a list of the characteristics of love described there. Memorize them and commit to incorporating them in your thoughts and actions toward others.

*"Love never fails"* (1 Corinthians 13:8).

▶ **Nurture** a dependence on the Lord.

*"Trust in the LORD with all your heart and lean not on your own understanding; in all your ways submit to him, and he will make your paths straight"* (Proverbs 3:5–6).

Many children who grow up in dysfunctional families enter adulthood with unresolved anger buried under a history of mistreatment and unmet emotional needs. For many, the connection between their present outbursts of anger and their past dysfunctional childhood is never seen. For others the cause and effect is not only seen and understood but becomes the springboard for change.

Taking the time to measure your current anger and connect it to your past is necessary for knowing how to tame your anger and keep it under control.

Have you seriously thought about *how much* anger you are holding inside your heart and *toward whom* you feel angry? See the following pie-shaped outline. Divide the pie into segments and put a specific name inside each segment to represent the amount of anger you feel toward the different people in your life (past or present). See the sample "Anger Pie," which shows general categories.[33]

As you think about your own anger, consider what the Bible says ...

> **"Human anger does not produce the
> righteousness that God desires."
> (James 1:20)**

# Sample Anger Pie

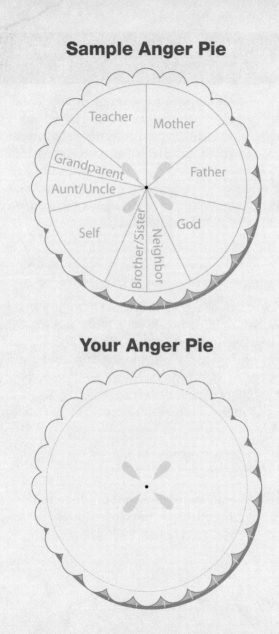

Teacher

Mother

Grandparent

Father

Aunt/Uncle

Self

God

Brother/Sister

Neighbor

# Your Anger Pie

# HOW TO Work Through Your Sorrow

Do you feel that your sorrow will never end, that your loss is a continual source of grief? Moving through the grief process takes time and commitment to "stay the course" until the goal of grief is accomplished—healing. Working through your grief is not an easy task; it is a difficult task that involves dedication. Be assured, God has a plan for you during this season of pain, and God will give you the strength to persevere through the pain.

**"You need to persevere so that when you have done the will of God, you will receive what he has promised." (Hebrews 10:36)**

▶ **Grief work** involves a step-by-step process through which a grieving person walks in order to reach a place of emotional healing.[34]

*"Though I walk in the midst of trouble, you preserve my life"* (Psalm 138:7).

▶ **Grief work**—*healthy* grief work—will culminate in ...[35]

- **Accepting** that the past will always be in the past
- **Accepting** that the present offers stability and significance
- **Accepting** that the future holds new and promising hope

In the end you can say, along with the apostle Paul ...

"We also glory in our sufferings, because we know that suffering produces perseverance; perseverance, character; and character, hope. And hope does not put us to shame, because God's love has been poured out into our hearts through the Holy Spirit, who has been given to us." (Romans 5:3–5)

## Grieving over Unforgiveness

QUESTION: "Someone close to me died, and now it is too late for me to ask forgiveness for what I did wrong. What can I do about my heavy guilt?"

ANSWER: You do not have to live with guilt even though the person you wronged is no longer available to you. Realize that God is available to you.

▶ **Write** down every wrong attitude and action. Then confess your sins to Him.

▶ **Ask** God's forgiveness, realizing that all sins (even against others) are sins against God because He has told us how we are to treat one another.

▶ **Write** a letter to the one you wronged, read it aloud, and ask God to forgive you on behalf of the other person.

God knows your heart, and He can forgive your sins and restore to you a clear conscience.

> **"Create in me a pure heart, O God, and renew a steadfast spirit within me. ... My sacrifice, O God, is a broken spirit; a broken and contrite heart you, God, will not despise."**
> **(Psalm 51:10, 17)**

## HOW TO Identify Unhealthy Family Roles

Children in dysfunctional families will often take on unhealthy roles.

▶ Children may *appear* one way on the outside, but *feel* something quite different on the inside. The "face" they put on for the family and others masks a deep pain they're afraid to express.

▶ They may perform certain *functions* in order to cope within the dysfunctional family structure.

▶ *Without emotional healing*, they may carry these harmful roles into adulthood and into their own family structures.

▶ *With emotional healing*, however, they can overcome their past and learn healthy boundaries and balances in life—and even use their past experiences to help others.

The following charts can help you identify these unhealthy family roles.

## The Hero

The responsible child, "golden child" (often the first child)

| | |
|---|---|
| They Appear | Incapable of making a mistake |
| They Feel | Afraid of failing |
| Their Function | Take over the parental role |
| Without Healing | Driven workaholics and compulsive perfectionists |
| With Healing | Aim for excellence while balancing work and play |
| They Appear | Do everything flawlessly |
| They Feel | Like failures because they can't fix the family |
| Their Function | Provide parents with proof that they are good parents |
| Without Healing | Riddled with stress |
| With Healing | Value enjoyment, more relaxed |
| They Appear | Performance oriented |
| They Feel | Never satisfied with anyone |
| Their Function | Instill a sense of family pride |
| Without Healing | No shame—believe the end justifies the means |
| With Healing | Become effective, ethical leaders |
| They Appear | Able to "do it all" |
| They Feel | Responsible to keep the family together and functioning |
| Their Function | Impart family worth |

| | |
|---|---|
| **Without Healing** | Seek significance based on what they do, not on who they are |
| **With Healing** | Take responsibility for self, not for everyone else |
| **They Appear** | Desirous of positive attention |
| **They Feel** | Detached from and unaware of their own emotions |
| **Their Function** | Enable the family to feel it has value through their successes |
| **Without Healing** | Self-professed failures because they can't change their families |
| **With Healing** | Accept individuality in each family member |
| **They Appear** | Superior in achievements |
| **They Feel** | Inadequate in every way |
| **Their Function** | Furnish a change of focus for the family away from its dysfunction |
| **Without Healing** | Self-sufficient and prideful |
| **With Healing** | Stress cooperative sharing, admit wrongs |
| **They Appear** | Mature and responsible |
| **They Feel** | Extreme shame over family dysfunction |
| **Their Function** | Prove to the world that their family is functional |
| **Without Healing** | Judgmental of others and themselves |
| **With Healing** | Accept failure as a part of life |

# The Scapegoat

The rebellious child, "black sheep"

| They Appear | Unable to do anything right |
|---|---|
| They Feel | Angry over the injustice they receive |
| Their Function | Take the focus off the dysfunctional parents |
| Without Healing | Irresponsible and don't care |
| With Healing | Accept responsibility willingly |
| They Appear | Inadequate |
| They Feel | Hostile over the hurt they endure from family members |
| Their Function | Provide distractions from real family issues |
| Without Healing | Addicts and prone to be prolific liars and troublemakers |
| With Healing | Possess the courage and discipline to change |
| They Appear | "Act out" family problems |
| They Feel | Enraged over the rejection they experience |
| Their Function | Receive blame for everything |
| Without Healing | Distrusting and cynical, but with a care-free attitude |
| With Healing | Accepting and fun-loving, "friend makers" |

| They Appear | Determined to cause trouble |
| --- | --- |
| They Feel | Believe even negative attention is better than no attention |
| Their Function | Give family cause to say, "If this child wasn't being a problem, we wouldn't have any problems." |
| Without Healing | Self-destructive, self-hatred |
| With Healing | Become the first in the family to enter a recovery program |
| They Appear | Defiant, strong-willed |
| They Feel | Compelled to confront family patterns of denial |
| Their Function | Allow the hero to be "good" since the scapegoat is "bad" |
| Without Healing | Judgmental, faultfinders |
| With Healing | Can become excellent counselors because of their empathy |
| They Appear | Irresponsible, self-destructive |
| They Feel | Dejected, like losers |
| Their Function | Carry all the family shame |
| Without Healing | Hopeless romantics with little discernment |
| With Healing | Honest and have a high regard for truth |

# The Lost Child

The reclusive child, "wall flower"

| | |
|---|---|
| **They Appear** | Quiet, unsociable, disinterested in family activities |
| **They Feel** | Ignored, like they don't fit in |
| **Their Function** | Enable the family to feel good about having a "no needs" child |
| **Without Healing** | Remain in denial about their feelings |
| **With Healing** | Can become skilled, compassionate listeners |
| **They Appear** | Shy, compliant, fragile |
| **They Feel** | Powerless, like a victim |
| **Their Function** | Provide relief for the family—"At least we don't have problems with this kid!" |
| **Without Healing** | Unwilling to formulate or share opinions |
| **With Healing** | Can be talented writers/actors/musicians who express their ideas through their writing, acting, and music |
| **They Appear** | Unmotivated, apt to procrastinate |
| **They Feel** | Like a nobody, unneeded, small and worthless yet see others as big and valuable |

| Their Function | Allow family to spend time on the "hero" and the "scapegoat" |
| --- | --- |
| Without Healing | Feel overlooked, like opportunity has passed them by |
| With Healing | Can be creative artists who express their hopes and dreams through their art |
| They Appear | Fearful of taking risks or engaging in competition |
| They Feel | Convinced that they must avoid conflict and intimacy for self-preservation |
| Their Function | Don't "rock the boat" in the family |
| Without Healing | Avoid activities that require intimate, social interaction |
| With Healing | Find ways to connect with people and form mutually, intimate relationships |
| They Appear | Lost in their thoughts, daydreamers |
| They Feel | Unable to express feelings— they don't know how they feel |
| Their Function | Make no emotional demands on the family |
| Without Healing | Not emotionally free to have meaningful relationships |
| With Healing | Develop relationships in which feelings are shared and valued |

# The Mascot

The reveling child, "clown" (often a younger child)

| | |
|---|---|
| **They Appear** | Friendly, have many friends |
| **They Feel** | Little self-worth |
| **Their Function** | "Social director" for the family |
| **Without Healing** | Involved in abusive relationships and "save" others |
| **With Healing** | Can become effective in the helping professions—social workers, therapists |
| **They Appear** | Accommodating, go with the flow |
| **They Feel** | False guilt, blame themselves even when they have done no wrong |
| **Their Function** | Take responsibility for the emotional well-being of family |
| **Without Healing** | Influenced too much by others, easily manipulated |
| **With Healing** | Learn how to lead, stand on principle |
| **They Appear** | Funny, cute, attract attention |
| **They Feel** | Scared of disapproval |
| **Their Function** | Provide comic relief for the family |
| **Without Healing** | Emotionally stuck, unable to grow up |
| **With Healing** | Kindhearted, generous, able to listen to others |

| They Appear | Hyperactive with a short attention span |
| --- | --- |
| They Feel | Inadequate, unequipped for life |
| Their Function | Distract family from problems |
| Without Healing | Unable to handle stress, may marry a "hero" to take care of them |
| With Healing | Take responsibility for their personal well-being |
| They Appear | People pleasers, attention seekers |
| They Feel | Unable to receive love, only give it |
| Their Function | Give the family a reason to lighten up |
| Without Healing | Expected to make others feel better even if it means ignoring their own pain |
| With Healing | Experience the full range of emotions |
| They Appear | Can't express difficult feelings |
| They Feel | Compelled to hide pain with humor |
| Their Function | Diffuse anger with laughter |
| Without Healing | Prone to make light of tragedy and suffering |
| With Healing | Use humor in healthy ways, possibly a professional entertainer |

"'For I know the plans I have for you,'
declares the LORD, 'plans to prosper you
and not to harm you,
plans to give you hope and a future.'"
(Jeremiah 29:11)

> *A poor background is*
> *a poor excuse for poor behavior.*
> *With the power of Christ within you,*
> *don't let your past overpower you.*
>
> —June Hunt

# SCRIPTURES TO MEMORIZE

In what ways can I show **love** when I don't feel loving toward my family?

> *"**Love** is patient, love is kind. It does not envy, it does not boast, it is not proud. ... it is not self-seeking, it is not easily angered, it keeps no record of wrongs."* (1 Corinthians 13:4–5)

Can I ever feel **secure** even though I came from such an insecure background?

> *"Whoever fears the LORD has a **secure** fortress, and for their children it will be a refuge."* (Proverbs 14:26)

How can I overcome the loss of not having a loving **father**?

> *"A **father** to the fatherless, a defender of widows, is God in his holy dwelling."* (Psalm 68:5)

How can I **be reconciled to** my family members who are difficult to get along with?

> *"If you are offering your gift at the altar and there remember that your brother or sister has something against you, leave your gift there in front of the altar. First go and **be reconciled to** them; then come and offer your gift."* (Matthew 5:23–24)

How can I get past responding out of my **childhood** pain?

*"When I was a child, I talked like a child, I thought like a child, I reasoned like a child. When I became a man, I put the ways of childhood behind me."* (1 Corinthians 13:11)

How can I **forgive** family members who have hurt me?

*"Bear with each other and forgive one another if any of you has a grievance against someone. Forgive as the Lord forgave you."* (Colossians 3:13)

Can God **heal** the deep **wounds** from my childhood?

*"He heals the brokenhearted and binds up their wounds."* (Psalm 147:3)

How can I break the bondage of living for the **approval of** other **people?**

*"Am I now trying to win the approval of human beings, or of God? Or am I trying to please people? If I were still trying to please people, I would not be a servant of Christ."* (Galatians 1:10)

My parents were not good role models for me. Whose **example** can I **follow** to be a more loving parent?

*"Follow God's example, therefore, as dearly loved children and walk in the way of love, just as Christ loved us and gave himself up for us as a fragrant offering and sacrifice to God."* (Ephesians 5:1–2)

How can I overcome bitterness toward those who **intended to harm me**?

*"You intended to harm me, but God intended it for good to accomplish what is now being done..."* (Genesis 50:20)

# NOTES

1. Rainbow Days, "About Us–Cathey Brown" (Dallas: Rainbow Days, 2011), http://www.rdikids.org/staff/catheybrown.html.

2. Cathey Brown, interview with June Hunt, *Hope for the Heart* radio program, January 8–12, 1990.

3. Brown, interview with June Hunt.

4. Bob Buford, *Finishing Well* (Grand Rapids: Zondervan, 2011), 204.

5. Jeff VanVonderen, *Tired of Trying to Measure Up* (Minneapolis, MN: Bethany House, 1989), 33.

6. Brown, interview with June Hunt.

7. Brown, interview with June Hunt.

8. Robert Hemfelt, Frank Minirth, and Paul Meier, *Love Is a Choice* (Nashville: Thomas Nelson, 1989), 157–59; H. Norman Wright, *Always Daddy's Girl: Understanding Your Father's Impact on Who You Are* (Ventura, CA: Regal, 1989), 163–71; Nancy LeSourd, *No Longer the Hero: The Personal Pilgrimage of an Adult Child* (Nashville:Thomas Nelson, 1991), 38–45.

9. Brown, interview with June Hunt.

10. Brown, interview with June Hunt.

11. Barbara Metzler, *Passionaries: Turning Compassion into Action* (West Conshohocken, PA: Templeton Press, 2006), 150–151.

12. Buford, *Finishing Well*, 204.

13. Brown, interview with June Hunt.

14. Buford, *Finishing Well*, 204–205.

15. David Field, *Family Personalities* (Eugene, OR: Harvest House, 1988), 19–29.

16. Brown, interview with June Hunt.

17. Brown, interview with June Hunt.

18. Brown, interview with June Hunt.

19. Buford, *Finishing Well*, 205.

20. Brown, interview with June Hunt.

21. Brown, interview with June Hunt.

22. Lawrence J. Crabb, Jr., *Understanding People: Deep Longings for Relationship*, Ministry Resources Library (Grand Rapids: Zondervan, 1987), 15–16; Robert S. McGee, *The Search for Significance*, 2nd ed. (Houston, TX: Rapha, 1990), 27–30.

23. Metzler, *Passionaries*, 151.

24. Metzler, *Passionaries*, 151.

25. Buford, *Finishing Well*, 205–206.

26. Brown, interview with June Hunt.

27. Nancy LeSourd, *No Longer the Hero*, 198–204.

28. Jim Conway, *Adult Children of Legal and Emotional Divorce: Healing Your Long-Term Hurt* (Downers Grove, IL: InterVarsity, 1990), 127–240.

29. LeSourd, *No Longer the Hero*, 173–74.

30. LeSourd, *No Longer the Hero*, 175–77.

31. Brown, interview with June Hunt.

32. David Mains, *Healing the Dysfunctional Church Family* (Wheaton, IL: Victor, 1992), 145–46.

33. Ronald T. Potter-Efron, *Angry All the Time: An Emergency Guide to Anger Control*, 2nd ed. (Oakland, CA: New Harbinger, 2005), 17.

34. H. Norman Wright, *Crisis Counseling: What to Do and Say During the First 72 Hours*, updated and expanded ed. (Ventura, CA: Regal, 1993), 158–159.

35. Wright, *Crisis Counseling*, 159–161.

# HOPE FOR THE HEART TITLES

- *Adultery*
- *Aging Well*
- *Alcohol & Drug Abuse*
- *Anger*
- *Anorexia & Bulimia*
- *Boundaries*
- *Bullying*
- *Caregiving*
- *Chronic Illness & Disability*
- *Codependency*
- *Conflict Resolution*
- *Confrontation*
- *Considering Marriage*
- *Critical Spirit*
- *Decision Making*
- *Depression*
- *Domestic Violence*
- *Dysfunctional Family*
- *Envy & Jealousy*
- *Fear*
- *Financial Freedom*
- *Forgiveness*
- *Friendship*
- *Gambling*
- *Grief*
- *Guilt*
- *Hope*
- *Loneliness*
- *Manipulation*
- *Marriage*
- *Overeating*
- *Parenting*
- *Perfectionism*
- *Procrastination*
- *Reconciliation*
- *Rejection*
- *Self-Worth*
- *Sexual Integrity*
- *Singleness*
- *Spiritual Abuse*
- *Stress*
- *Success Through Failure*
- *Suicide Prevention*
- *Trials*
- *Verbal & Emotional Abuse*
- *Victimization*

**www.hendricksonrose.com**